ZOOM IN ON DRAGONFLIES

Melissa Stewart

E Enslow Elementary

CONTENTS

WORDS TO KNOW

antennae (an TEN ee)— Two long, thin body parts on the head of insects and some other animals. Antennae help animals sense the world around them.

claspers (KLAS puhrz)—The two body parts a male dragonfly uses to grab a female while they mate.

nymph (NIMF)—The second part in the life cycle of some insects. A nymph changes into an adult.

prey (PRAY)—An animal that is hunted for food.

DRAGONFLY HOMES

ZOOM BUBBLE

Dragonflies have lived on Earth for millions of years. You can find them near most ponds and streams. In places where winter is cold, some dragonflies fly to warmer areas.

PARTS OF A DRAGONFLY

wing

thorax

eye

abdomen

claspers

leg

DRAGONFLY BODY

ZOOM BUBBLE

A dragonfly is an insect. An insect has six legs. Its body has three parts. An insect's head is in the front. The thorax is in the middle. The abdomen is the part at the back.

DRAGONFLY WINGS

ZOOM BUBBLE

Dragonflies have two sets of wings. They can fly as fast as a car drives on the highway.
Dodge! Dart!
Whiz! Whirl!
The long, tough wings carry the insect through the air.

DRAGONFLY MOUTH

ZOOM BUBBLE

A dragonfly eats small flying insects. It catches its meaty meals in the air. Then it pops them into its mouth. A dragonfly chews its prey with its strong jaws.

This dragonfly has just caught a bee.

DRAGONFLY LEGS

ZOOM BUBBLE

A dragonfly has six legs. They are attached to the middle of its body.

The insect flies with its legs bunched together. The legs form a basket that scoops up prey.

13

DRAGONFLY EYES

ZOOM BUBBLE

A dragonfly has two huge eyes. They are the best eyes in the insect world.

The eyes can see right and left, up and down, all at the same time! They help the hungry hunter spot flying prey.

15

DRAGONFLY ANTENNAE

ZOOM BUBBLE

Can you see this dragonfly's antennae? They are tiny. And they don't do much. They can't feel or hear or taste. They can smell things, but not very well.

DRAGONFLY CLASPERS

ZOOM BUBBLE

When a male dragonfly spots a female, he grabs her. He uses claspers on the back of his body. The two insects lock their bodies and fly through the air. This is how they mate.

This nymph is
shedding its skin.

DRAGONFLY NYMPHS

ZOOM BUBBLE

When a dragonfly comes out of its egg, it has no wings. Its body is short. The **nymph** has to live in the water for two or three years. Then it crawls onto land. It sheds its skin and becomes an adult.

LIFE CYCLE

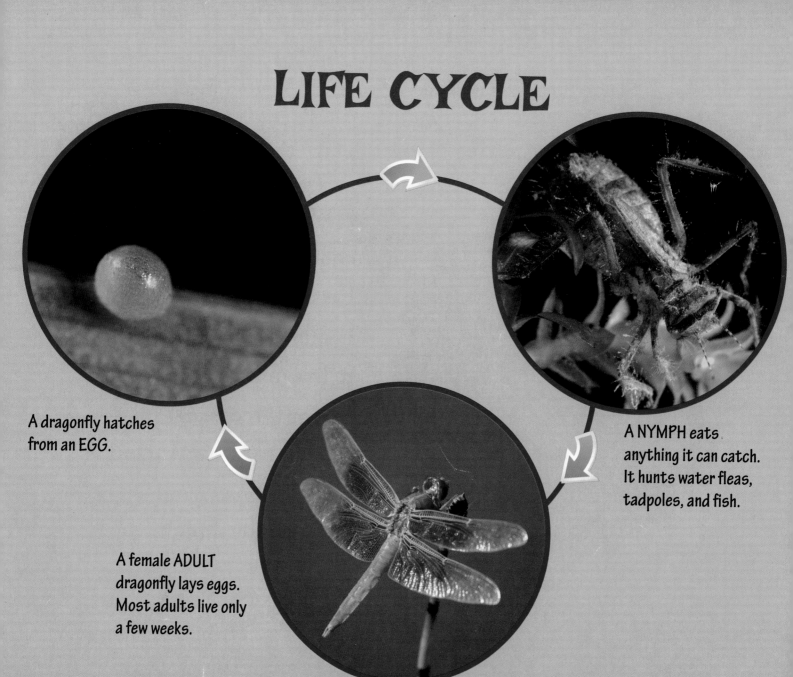

A dragonfly hatches from an EGG.

A NYMPH eats anything it can catch. It hunts water fleas, tadpoles, and fish.

A female ADULT dragonfly lays eggs. Most adults live only a few weeks.

LEARN MORE

BOOKS

Nelson, Robin. *Dragonflies*. Minneapolis: Lerner, 2009.

Peters, Elisa. *It's a Dragonfly!* New York: PowerKids Press, 2008.

St. Pierre, Stephanie. *Dragonfly*. Chicago: Heinemann Library, 2008.

WEB SITES

Dragonfly
  <http://kids.sandiegozoo.org/animals/insects/dragonfly>

Tracking Migration of Dragonflies, Sparrows, and Bees
  <http://www.nationalgeographic.com/explorers/projects/tracking-animal-migration/#/attaching-device-to-dragonfly_25903_600x450.jpg>

INDEX

Enslow Elementary, an imprint of Enslow Publishers, Inc.
Enslow Elementary® is a registered trademark of Enslow Publishers, Inc.

Copyright © 2014 by Melissa Stewart

Library of Congress Cataloging-in-Publication Data

Stewart, Melissa.

Zoom in on dragonflies / Melissa Stewart.

p. cm. — (Zoom in on insects!)

Summary: "Provides information for readers about a dragonfly's home, food, and body"—Provided by publisher.

Includes index.

ISBN 978-0-7660-4212-4

1. Dragonflies—Juvenile literature. I. Title. II. Series: Stewart, Melissa. Zoom in on insects.

QL520.S755 2014

595.733—dc23

2012040388

Future editions:

Paperback ISBN: 978-1-4644-0367-5

EPUB ISBN: 978-1-4645-1203-2

Single-User PDF ISBN: 978-1-4646-1203-9

Multi-User PDF ISBN: 978-0-7660-5835-4

Printed in the United States of America

102013 Lake Book Manufacturing, Inc. Melrose Park, IL

10 9 8 7 6 5 4 3 2 1

Series Literacy Consultant:
Allan A. De Fina, PhD
Past President of the New Jersey Reading Association
Dean, College of Education
New Jersey City University
Jersey City, New Jersey

Science Consultant:
Helen Hess, PhD
Professor of Biology
College of the Atlantic
Bar Harbor, Maine

Photo Credits: © iStockphoto.com/Margo van Leeuwen, p. 10; © Dwight Kuhn, p. 22 (egg, nymph); Mark Beckwith/Photos.com, p. 18; Oliver Anlauf/Photos.com, p. 1; Pavel Lebedinsky/Photos.com, p. 13; Rene Krekels/Foto Natura/Minden Pictures, p. 20; Richard Becker/FLPA/Minden Pictures, p. 12; Shuttertock.com, pp. 2, 3, 4, 6, 7, 8, 9, 11, 15, 16, 17, 19, 21, 22 (adult); Sopon Phikanesuan/Photos.com, p. 14; Zaliha Yussof/Photos.com, p. 5.

Cover Photo: Oliver Anlauf/Photos.com

Enslow Elementary
an imprint of
Enslow Publishers, Inc.
40 Industrial Road
Box 398
Berkeley Heights, NJ 07922
USA
http://www.enslow.com